Meat and Bone

Poems by Sandra Feen

Luchador Press
Big Tuna, TX

Copyright © Sandra Feen, 2019
First Edition1 3 5 7 9 10 8 6 4 2
ISBN: 978-1-950380-56-5
LCCN: 2019948038

Design, edits and layout: El Dopa
Cover image: R. Nikolas Macioci
Author photo: Penny Thieme
All rights reserved. No part of this publication may be reproduced or transmitted in any form or by any means, electronic or mechanical, including photocopying, recording or by info retrieval system, without prior written permission from the author.

The author would like to thank the editors of the following publications where some of these poems originally appeared:

Pudding House Publications: "Hey Good Lookin',"
Redkitchen Poetry Troupe Anthology: "Able Movers," "Stuffed Glass," and "Three Old Ladies and a Poet"
Winner of Columbus Arts Festival Spoken Word Competition: "Stuffed Glass"
The Ohio State University's Summer Magazine: "Able Movers"

TABLE OF CONTENTS

Refusal / 1

Meeting: A Trilogy / 2

Meeting Your Mother / 6

Engagement at Key West / 7

A Day's Colon Blow and Morphine Shot / 9

Keeping the Veil On / 12

Most and Least / 15

And If I Had but One / 16

No Fire / 17

Left / 21

In Fall / 23

Mad / 25

Able Movers / 28

Three Old Ladies and a Poet / 30

Valentine-less / 32

The Day Your Visa Bill / 34

A Woman Named Monique / 35

Stuffed Glass / 37

The Painter / 40

As Is / 42

Odd Pair / 44

A Matter of Semantics / 47

The Key In / 48

In Grandpa's Cellar / 50

Incoming Male / 52

You Still Married? / 54

An Average Woman's Addiction to Chocolate / 56

Divorced Girl's Rant / 58

1991 AIDS Test Debacle / 59

Content / 62

Lost Suitcase / 64

Meat and Bone / 66

Thirteen Years Later / 70

Complex / 71

Strange Things / 73

June 3 / 75

Mockery of Mourning / 77

Calling Hours / 79

Epilogue / 81

FINAL EPILOGUE / 82

For Susan S., for beginning a friendship with Jane at age eight and twenty years later, holding her hand in a courtroom.

For Kim S., for suggesting that the book be dedicated to 26-year-old Jane. I extend that dedication to all young women and men in their twenties, as it can be a harrowing time period for a multitude of reasons.

Finally, for Judy B., with immense love and respect.

Beside you...
What is all this?
I know how furiously your heart is beating.

-Wallace Stevens
from "Gray Room"

Refusal

She's home from college
a weekend, sleeping in.
Mom shakes her awake.

Sam, she sometimes called
her, *Get yourself all dolled up!*
Dad's young friend is here.

He's so handsome, sweet!
They teach history together
at night school. Wake up!

Are you kidding? Meet
an old fogie friend of Dad's?
Sorry, I refuse.

Meeting: A Trilogy

I.
I am a substitute teacher after graduating college.
East is the first high school to call. I'm scared
and Mom, elated, her first thought that I really must look you up
while I'm there – I've no excuse not to.
During a class change on my conference period, after kids tell
    me your room number, 132, I head there to introduce myself.
I squint, frustrated I don't have my glasses with me.
Surely the gorgeous man standing outside his classroom door
welcoming students can't be you!
Indeed, you belong to the blonde hair and
blue eyes, and my interior monologue marvels,
unapologetically; *Wow. You're Dad's friend.* Your warmth and
    courtesy
speak briefly to me – you're sure we'll meet again.

II.
And we do,
when I'm hired to teach adult evening high school,
and you, the assistant principal, stop by my room each evening
to make sure I have everything I need.
I'm in my early twenties teaching literature classes, ages 16 to 65,
a challenging, but comfortable bliss, in one of the oldest schools
    in Clintonville —
my favorite part of the city. The carved wood, tall windows, grand
as my eagerness to be greeted by your gentlemanly approach:

Salutations and goodbyes seem to lengthen a little. As weeks
wear on, I get to school a little earlier, leave a bit later.
Enthusiasm consumes you when I say I heard about your love
　　for scuba diving –
how it takes you to tropical, exotic places.
You veer closer, ask about my love for poetry:
I hear you're a poet. I'd like to see your poems sometime,
and you ask me which poets I love, and I carry on about
　　Cummings, Piercy,
then you mention Yeats with passion, and I respond yes, in
　　breathless agreement,
then you shift into a quick tangent about Hemingway,
Gertrude Stein, and a swift transition back to other subjects I love:
antiques, abstract expressionism, and the renaissance you tantalize,
your aura hums vibrating my tongue, and I swallow, yet

my day job consumes me. Teaching over a hundred students
effectively is where my evaluation rests, whether a career
continues. I drag heavier into teaching at day's end.
I must give up its euphoria, imprison time with grading,
　　snatches of sleep.
My final night, I walk briskly out, cocoon myself in the car
to contain tears, think I'll never see you again.

III.
But the following school year, you walk through those open
　　library doors
our first meeting day. You were staff reduced hours before
from a Peer Assistant Review Program,
your day time administrative position,
and assigned to my high school to teach history.

You see me see you immediately; I'm nervous
jubilance. You smile, look into my eyes,
say something without words, or at least I crave to believe this.

Third period comes, our first day of school with students.
I'm kicked out of my room, as are you, so others
can teach in our spaces. We're marooned in the teacher's lounge.
and no one else with the same conference period.
Talking is conveniently private, routine for weeks,

then Christmas break takes you to scuba diving adventures in
New Guinea, and when you return, you lean from behind my
chair third period, and over my left shoulder, touching it,
dangle black coral earrings in front of my face and say,
I bring you a piece of New Guinea.
I weight your gift significant, with hope it symbolizes
something, hope a clairvoyant would deem these dark stones
synchronistic, part of the line of order: That your staff reduction
brings you here, sitting across from me in a narrow island of calm,
in a bedlam building. That this jewelry that now dangles
from my earlobes is durable keepsake marking the start of years
   of tables
to come where we will sit, face each other,

and I decide; I must make this happen.
I ask you to meet me in German Village the following
Friday, the first one in January.
I tell you to bring your pictures from your trip.

We'll have dinner and wine, and I'll enjoy story after story.
(We don't miss a Friday or Saturday from then on, right into our Friday rehearsal and Saturday wedding the following October.)

You ask me next, as I thought you would, though more a declaration.
You tell me to come over for pizza the following January Friday to your home.
We watch your favorite movie, *The Unbearable Lightness of Being* a movie quite prophetic.

Meeting Your Mother

We arrive in Eustis, at Lake Ridge Village.
She had you at 40 and will soon turn 80.

You call her kid.
Kid, this is Jane.

She grips my right arm, insists,
*Come out with me to my back yard
and pick an orange. We'll eat it right there
and let the juice roll down to our elbows.
Don't mind the snakes.*

Engagement at Key West

Vintage emerald ring
bought, you ask Dad permission
then on one knee, me.

After yes, we fly
to Eustis, to meet your Mom
then drive to Key West.

Endure AIA
from Key Largo to Key West,
I snorkel, get stung

by jelly fish, itch
ignites, after bottle of
meat tenderizer

poured on my burnt breasts
on board boat, later behind
menu hide, to scratch

at Jimmy Buffet's.
Hit every island bookstore,
reach Check Point Charlie.

We're engagement bliss.
Brooding weather, briskly
we enter the Café

Exile for dinner,
as wind reaps outside mayhem.
We write a mystery,

use hyperbole
enjoy wine and ominous
clouds. Romance flows.

Then the lights go out
in Café Exile. Abrupt.
The island blinks black.

Hand in hand we tip-
toe best we can without sight
and keep our mystery

going, flinging
lines back and forth while thunder
bawls, frenzy of rain

managing our way
back to Hotel La Te Da
relishing this night

wet, amorous, dark,
savoring unexpected
rush. Forget flashlight.

A Day's Colon Blow and Morphine Shot

You think you will die
in the parking lot of that luxury hotel.
That is, die in your shit you unload
as soon as you open the jeep door
and pull down your plaid shorts in
the knick of stinking time, while I sit
in the passenger seat and close my eyes,
pray Key West cops won't come,
pray screams, gasps, and gags will quickly
subside from the wedding party passing; they
think they're going to take pictures, bridesmaids,
grooms stagger strategically on steps of a tropical veranda.

The tighter I close my eyes, the louder you moan
in the muck of your dump, and sharper the cries
of shock, disdain. You have no idea what brings
on this gurgling turmoil violating your intestines
that exorcise your steering wheel into a parking lot—
not a gas station, but a luxury hotel to leave a dark
mound of excrement in between freshly painted lines
of space reserved for expectant mothers.

When your bowels become a ghost town, the parking
lot is too, with only flies left in attendance, feasting.

We vanish before police come,
hope no one records our license number, but
we never escape your smell the rest of the day; it
resides in the walls of the car, the seat belts, your arms,
torso, fingernails, hair, no matter how fiercely
you scrub back in our room at La Te Da.

You try to dismiss your ordeal, as your stomach
settles down, and I lean forward, brush
my hair thoroughly since you insist
I should try on dresses at the nearest boutique.
I lift from the last brush stroke, hear something crunch
in my back. Like shells, it nearly knocks the wind out,
sends a swift searing bullet of pain up my back, down
my left arm to pinch my elbow, and reverse its course
back to target my buttocks.

I don't want to complain, especially when your cologne
still doesn't cover up the stubborn stench of (that) fecal
matter. You sweetly say taking me on this outing helps you forget.
You bring skirts and dresses in profusion to my dressing
room door, and I can barely maneuver them onto my body.

After deciding to wear a matching green linen
blouse and skirt that you chose back to the hotel,
it is then that I inform you of the hurricane
of pain raging under my shoulder blades.

You insist I try to nap, but misery clamps
me there with a vengeance until I can't get up;
it forces you to pull my legs forward to get the best
hold on me, carry me to the car, drive, then repeat grip,
lift, and carry me into the emergency room.

I'm in a twin bed leaning on my right elbow,
keeping weight away from my butt that doctors
say is swollen. How can something so
balloon-like, so round know the science of growing
swollen, as well? They inject morphine
directly into the left cheek of the bubble. It doesn't
pop, but I yelp, and a six-year-old one cubicle over
pulls the curtain back, asks if I'm the one who just made that noise.

When he finds out the shot is the culprit provoking me,
he states matter-of-factly he's been poked earlier,
hadn't uttered a speck of noise. The kid is cool like he's been around
and in and out of many curtained cubicles, until his Mom
accuses him of neglecting to make regular stops to the restroom
and his paper gown bristles. This comment makes you slink
farther away from the kid, slither through the curtain to realign closer
to my bed. Morphine creates a fog that allows me to breathe easier.
Although less concerned about the needled reek of today
I'm reminded that you still need yet another scrub.

Keeping the Veil On

It is a late October wedding.
A long, traditional reception of dancing follows
after tossing tradition down the aisle: I wear a
backless, deep ivory dress. Yes. Backless, but
when we leave the reception, I change
into jeans and a button up red sweater to
get to the hotel but keep my veil on. I love
the quirky looks I get from bystanders, and
surprisingly, you get such a kick out of them too.
14 years younger than you, I occasionally bring
the playful out of you, help you
worry less about appearances,
reject decorum. We skip hand in hand
in the parking garage of downtown Columbus'
Holiday Inn, and when we enter our hotel room,
you see to it that two dozen scarlet roses
wait inside.

I plan every bit of how I will look, be.
I'll smell of *Red* perfume that you gave to me
last Spring, I'll feel extra smooth to caress.
I plan what I'll say, how I'll move to touch your love
this night, our night, our bed of marriage.

You say, why not keep the veil on, but it is
uncomfortable and lying on a dozen stiff bobby pins

is prison. I pull it off, with difficulty,
get up, prepare, prepare, prepare,
return to hug into you, try to kiss you
but you brush my lips so quick and light, it tickles.

I don't feel you fall a deep lush fall into my
embrace, but a union begins anyway and I am happy
but in the middle of your thrush, you stop.
A major halt, the way one rides a bike free and clear
on a perfect day of weather, but the front wheel meets a rock
and I don't see it coming, so blinded by sun and breeze
fuzzing my bangs. I brace myself, nearly fall off,

and I gulp air, ask what's wrong; your voice is soft, soothing,
say nothing's wrong but that it is time to call your
mother to make sure she is all right, and you do swiftly,
in quiet urgency as if common, earnest duty.
You exchange pleasantries, get assurance all is well
and I whisper a reminder my parents will be over
to see her at noon the next day, take her to brunch,
and our honeymoon consists of a mere two days –
your mother will still be there when we return.
Noon is not now, you say, in firm resignation,
then once your conversation ends, hand me the phone,
say it is my time to call my parents. I quip, an incredulous
no thank you, then when you ask why not, just
as bewildered, I try to put a hammer to the head of
my sarcasm, say without tone that there is no way they
will want to hear from me. A call from me now will
only alarm them.

You don't press me or retort, but after using
the bathroom, return to bed, say it's time
to go to sleep. After all everything is exhausting.

I ask God in my head to help me with whatever
I'm about to face,
as I lie in the dark with my eyes open.

Most and Least

What do you love the most about me?
How much you care.
What do you love the least about me?
How much you care.

And if I had but one

delicious kiss my
lips lost in yours tossed
on a new bright white
brass iron bed bought
for a new bright white
marriage kiss passion
not goodnight not a curtain-
closer let's calm down potion
sleep peck tranquilizer but
a purple grape plop love
squeezer eye-opener lip
plunger arouser then
surprise you, grant your goodnight
take your so long shift to
true dreams too sweet not
flop and mumble breathless cries
of why I'm not your princess fire.

No Fire

Where are the matches? She wonders nervously as she looks up at the kitchen clock. *Only ten more minutes, and I can't even find the matches! The candles must be lit when he comes through the door. They just have to.* She fast-forwards around the room, checking everything off her mind's to-do list. Every room was dusted and vacuumed, strawberries on the glass coffee table in his treasured Weller bowl, the fireplace lit, and his favorite George Winston piano CD playing. The table was set with mauve and gray linens to match their yet-to-be-used Noritake Etienne wedding china. *On top of the cleanser!* she announces to her cat lounging on the white kitchen tile. She laughs, races upstairs to the bathroom. She often places things in obscure spots. Her husband says she did it at least seven times last month. She grabs the matches on top of the Comet next to the Windex on the sink, opens the bathroom cupboard to put away the cleaning supplies. Her birth control pills sandwiched between dust rags startle her. She swallows one quickly, thinking that maybe tonight, on their six-month anniversary she really will feel newly-wed. She stares at herself in the mirror, turns right, left, decides that the tummy flattening panties her mother bought her will make him really adore her in the long white lace nightie. She stops her swaying when she hears the grind of the garage door.

    She races down six-carpeted steps two at a time, lights candles finally, then checks the fire under the chicken stir-fry.

Hi little Sadie, Lee says as he picks up their calico.

Hi Honey. She approaches her husband, tries to kiss his lips while she stands tiptoe next to his 6'2 frame, but he buries his mouth in the cat's fur and she lands his cheek instead.

Aren't you cold in that? he muses while Sadie jumps from his arms. He loosens his tie and unbuttons the top of his starched white shirt.

No, not at all.

You must be cold or you wouldn't have a fire going. It's April and you have a fire going?

I just thought it would be nice for you to come home to a romantic fire, she says softly, twisting a long strand of her wavy auburn hair.

It's too much trouble, he responds, walking up the stairs.

What are you doing?

What do you think I'm doing? I'm getting out of these clothes. Why don't you put on a sweater or your flannel robe, dear? he yells from their bedroom. *You know how easily you catch colds.* Just then the phone rings. She knows it's 10:05. His friend Wes calls every night exactly ten minutes after he arrives home. Wes is Lee's best friend and was the best man in their wedding. *Get the phone!* Lee yells from the bathroom.

Good evening, Wes.

Well, aren't you a smart lady! Is the man of the house available?

No, he's not. The woman of the house has cooked a special dinner. It's our sixth month anniversary. Lee will have to call you ba—

I've got it, Lee speaks from the phone in his upstairs office. *Hey boy, what's up?* She hangs up the receiver before hearing their usual laughter. She gives them five minutes, then walks to the opening of his office, to remind Lee that dinner is waiting. Whispers replace his boisterous tone. She returns to the dining room table, sits, winces, allows pink candle wax to drip and collect on her left forefinger.

Suddenly her shoulders tense. *Did I remember to put the bottle of pills back behind the books?* She had found a white bottle that was foreign to her, while dusting his bookcase. She couldn't pronounce the main word on the label, but the others-- *strengthen, energize,* and *enhance sexual performance* -- made sense to her. She yells, *Are you off the phone yet? Dinner's definitely ready!* Ten minutes later, Lee responds by running down the stairs -- two at a time -- in a Cleveland Browns t-shirt and faded gray sweatpants.

Why don't you put the food in the freezer and we'll save it for when Mom comes to visit, or even nuke it tomorrow? I'm tired and ready to go to bed.

But it's only 10:30. You've hardly been home a half-hour. You haven't eaten! It's our sixth month anniversary, her voice rising.

I realize that. Don't you think I realize things? I'm a busy man, a tired one. You have no idea how tired I am.

I don't think you realize anything about me, or you, or us. When are you going to wake up? She's strident now.

I can't wake up until I've had some sleep, he says chuckling, reaching for the strawberry bowl. *Why don't you throw the food in the fridge and get some sleep with me? I'll bet you haven't even gotten your papers graded tonight.* He plops one strawberry whole in his mouth, puts down the bowl, and skips stairs again, on an upward climb. She turns her back to him, faces the pair of abstract paintings her sister and brother-in-law jointly created as a wedding present for them. Her chocolate eyes fix on the swirl of red and purple hues, vibrant, dancing in unison above the stark white sofa. Within seconds, she knows he is already in bed. He is lying on his side, hands tucked far under his pillow. His back faces her side of the bed. One foot is purposely exposed from under the pink and cream comforter. He says two feet under make him panic.

    She breaks her thoughts with quick, precise movement. She runs into the kitchen, grabs the skillet handle with her right hand, simultaneously opens the refrigerator door with her left, and places the hot skillet on the top shelf. She retrieves the salad and bottle of Hungarian wine, placing them also in the refrigerator. The rest of the table is left untouched.

    She digs both nails of her forefingers into her thumb cuticles, labors every step to the dark bedroom, and begins, *Do you know how tired I am? I'm tired of being told to go to sleep a half-hour after you get home. I'm tired of how much you work. I'm tired of you spending more time talking to the best man than you do your bride. We are still newlyweds! I don't even know what that means! I'm tired of begging to be loved and wondering what else I can try to fix on and in myself to make me more loveable.*

    Did you say something? Lee says through a yawn as he rolls over towards her still standing by the bed. *You put everything in the freezer, didn't you? Did you put out the fire?"*

Left

I liked being the only left-handed
person in my family.
In third grade I didn't fear
Mrs. Hunt's threats to tie
my hand behind my back
unless I earned an A in penmanship.
With tight defiance I clutched
my fat pencil, while she warned me
that the left hand
is the devil's hand.

Twenty years later, after one year
he decides he just can't
be married. I can
barely lift my hand
hold a fork or use my favorite pen.
My left hand is a well
that cups all my pain.
Each conversation with him
fills it with new wounds
reminds it of old bruises.

What creates this extensive throb?
the weight of a wedding band
and engagement ring
from a man who long overlooked
and discarded his symbol?

The memory of his squeezing
my hand roughly
pushing me down
or the abuse of his own hands
ripping off the door jamb
punching holes in the wall?
Do my fingertips press loss
when I pick up his wedding present?
I want my new wife to have
the best when she writes, he said.
I adore and use his pen
but my left-hand tires
with the agony of
writing this.

In Fall

You erase conversations
with parents that Open House night
words blur into bulletin board paint:
not one stiff smile, not one face
in hallway connects,

then principal's intercom voice,
punctilious, instructs *go home.*
Your pain runs with quick high heels
attentive to parking lot concrete
to car, leaf-pistoled,
chilled as car key
shaking fingers, thumb, place
in ignition, and steering wheel turns
sluggish, traffic lights green-beckon
awkward climate: enter that office
turn its smooth, steel doorknob
to small space of one man
having firmed tales, oblong
other certain he can make him
come in time for first anniversary,
if he could figure out why you, woman,
exert so much pressure
so much pressure, in flex
arms of high-backed chair, clutch

bicycle handles, unbend January ride
and ache, back, stuck on frigid vinyl block
and eyes of this counselor bite, swim all over
and into your body and husband's eyes avoid every inch
particularly your own eyes: truth
too rigid to bear.

Mad

Mad is the mother who kicks her
child over every inch of
his body and orders him not
to feel. Mad is the mother
who kicks until his screams
flee under the table
and she pulls the table from
the wall with ease as if she were drawing
curtains. She collars and impounds him
again and again, nails him so good he buries
it until 42. And like a nail, it suddenly resurfaces,
after working its way out over time, he panics,
pounds it back in place, runs to the bathroom
as refuge, locks the door, barring a wife
and her comfort.

Mad is the mother who wants
the best for her child and wants
to sabotage the best at the same time.
She says she likes his third fiancé
the best of them all, she has
a feeling in her gut that this
one will work, but wife better
not cross her, she warns,
and she comes for the wedding

writes in her journal that this
one was the most beautiful
and stays after the wedding
long after the wedding
calls them at Inn at Honey Run
on their two-day honeymoon. When they
return home to her
they open their wedding gifts. She watches.

She tells this wife to put something more
on, when he comes home late from work – she'll
catch cold in something so skimpy.
She's a mad mother, mad mother is mad,
Madmother insists on making his dinner
and when wife cleans up, he whispers to her to
keep quiet, without explanation
and when they all retire upstairs,
continues *Mother's a light sleeper so we
shouldn't have sex – we can't
let her hear us.* When Madmother finally
leaves, they argue about her visit.

Two months later, they vacation to her home.
She bangs on their door when they sleep past 8:00am,
turns the radio volume louder, louder.

Once Madmother hovered over their guest bed, staring.
Wife wakes up, grabs comforter, lets out
a combination scream/gasp, asks Madmother if she's all right.

26

Madmother says nothing to disrupt her own stare, so wife rouses her husband, amazed the commotion hasn't already stirred him, says she opened her eyes to his Madmother's stiff stance over their bed, her face fixed in an earnest, unbreakable stare and he mutters, THAT's *what you woke me up for?*
She does that all the time.

Mad is the mother the wife hears shaming her son, hears her telling him his back is ugly. He should never take off his shirt.

Madmother expects a call every Sunday.
Wife thinks this is Madmother's one reasonable request, reminds husband to make the call, that maybe Madmother will soften to the pattern of his ring. He calls wife a nag – he procrastinates – she becomes her own mad when he doesn't. When his barometer bottoms out, he calls Madmother, melts completely into her, tone soft, pressure balances whispering complacency, tells her profusely how much he loves her.

Madmother wants to come for three weeks during her son's second married Christmas together. Wife calls, pleads for a delayed visit, or at least a shortened one. Wife breaks down, admits she and Madmother's son have problems—that they need vacation from their teaching schedules to save them.
Mad is the mother who matter-of- factly asks if it's
a sexual problem — accentuates *seeexxxuualll.*
Says he wanted to tell his father something about his identity, on his father's deathbed; his dad died before those words were uttered.

Madmother calls the next day; her plane ticket is bought.

Able Movers

They come a day late.
Their driver got thrown in jail
the morning before.
On an 8:00am Sunday
I hear howling, a pack of wolves
fierce in their heat. I look out the window,
see three disheveled men
jump out onto our lawn
from a white truck marked *Able*.
Darol's in charge, the one
with charcoal braids touching his toosh
and three tongues tattooed
between his open denim vest.
Able Movers at your service!
he yells brazen enough for our friends
six doors down to hear.
Mick is a beach-boy-bell-bottom-blonde
and Hal doesn't say much, just
informs me right away that he's new
on the job. His buddies woke him up
a half hour ago, and he excuses
himself for not wearing a shirt
or being too friendly, but he's still hung over
from the night, before.
They begin lifting

the wrong furniture, not comprehending
that his furniture stays
and mine goes.
Them's antiques, ain't they?
Mick asks, tapping his dirt-coated fingernail
on my grandmother's trunk. I nod,
return a smile, my head buzzing a panic of prayers.
When I leave, the neighbors' eyes
are fixed on this fiasco.
The trio tail me to the cubbyhole
where I am to live, try to be
careful with the Czech glass collection.
They say this job is an easy one,
but they're still surprised I'm moving
from a home into an apartment
and why, wonders Darol, would I
clutter my crib with so many
damn boxes of books?
It was our pleasure to serve you,
they chant with last night's dinner
and a Budweiser breakfast on
stubborn breath; they wouldn't object if I gave
the big boss a call, spew out
immense praises.
They leave as fast as I can
plead the last one out the door,
pleased to make a few quick bucks
off somebody's problem.

Three Old Ladies and a Poet

When I was single
I frequented The Golden Hobby Shop.
I laughed at the dozens of matching coasters and houses
lining the shelves.
Each house's chimney shot up tissue.

Crocheted coaster and tissue
houses line the bay windows
of my neighborhood.
Mine philodendron and a calico.

Myrtle and Doris and Isabelle's apartments
smell like mothballs,
cinnamon cookies, Ben Gay,
Ivory soap.
Mine smells like textbooks,
Rax French fries, kitty litter
Red perfume.

They are friendly
and like living next to a schoolteacher.
They are also curious
about the two last names on my mailbox,
but seem afraid to question.
I am private
for the first time in my life.

Our ages add up to 263
and I am 28 of those numbers
amused by our differences,
and like the contrast of our little homes
tucked away on one floor of a building
on Roxbury Road, in a village called
Marble Cliff.

Valentine-less

I ask you to come over after night school
for a Valentine's dinner. I am counting
on your words holding weight, authenticity
when you said our separation is temporary,
so I try to speed up my return home.

I use a vintage lace tablecloth, our wedding china,
buy gifts I know you'll love. I'm wearing a short
satin red skirt and white silk blouse.
You won't be happy that my hair is longer, so
I wear it up.

I throw heart confetti all over the table
and recall the first night I slept in this
one-bedroom apartment:
I washed my hair, twisted it up in a towel
then unwound it, threw the towel on
the middle of the living room floor.
It felt like the greatest act of liberation
after living in close confinement and a strict
regiment for months.

Tonight, I light candles, blow them out, relight, blow,
reheat food, wait, wait.
You finally show up, two hours late.
You had been at a bar, you say.

You ask to use the bathroom, then come
out and hand me a card. When you eat,
you insist on standing. You politely
thank me for your gifts

wrap up the evening quickly, kiss
my forehead, leave.

I use my bathroom, find
a Kroger bag with a receipt
for a card on the floor.

The Day Your Visa Bill

came to my mailbox labeled
my name, your accident
I was relieved that
I don't have the burden
of paying for two dozen florist bouquets
and dinners, nightcaps, and hotels.

I wonder who she
or he
is.

A Woman Named Monique

As soon as you sweep the remaining dust of me out the door
and my voice skids down our driveway,
I find odd comfort reverberating between
newly painted walls of an apartment I still
do not claim as mine. Then a woman named Monique calls.

She's a big wheel from our urban city schools where we make
our career, with a title longer than what will ever capture my
interest or acceptance. She's #2 or #3 in charge to the
    superintendent,
a deputy something or other, maybe some loftier sounding name
given to a woman shipped in from another state to puff up
    the uppermost
power, and somehow the two of you meet, since you climbed

administrative curricular ranks, and every teacher knows
in this system, the higher the succession and longer the label,
the less authentic, helpful to those with that single named, daily
on-the-front-line position, the *teacher*.

She informs me she first called my parents and asked for my
    number.
When Mom refused to give it to the Audacious, she snatches
    it from my personnel folder.
She could have easily gotten it there to begin with.

What pleasure did she have announcing to them the nature of
    her relationship with you —
you and your double indemnity of lovers —
and our lawyers haven't even pronounced us legally dead

yet. But your tryst with Monique is starting to sour or she
    wouldn't have called,
she admits, and she begins a litany of questions about when our
    rotting began,
and whether you have problems with intimacy.
She never asks a single question about your roommate.

I say firmly I'm not in the business of trashing you,

and she quips I needn't cop an immediate attitude. When she
    sees my vein won't open for revenge, she throws in a random
comment as a final after-thought:

*You know, he's real protective of that silly little thing you made him
    for your first anniversary,
your only anniversary, right? Like's it's sacred or something. You
know how you framed his favorite Yeats poem? What was that –
wrapping paper from wedding gifts that you used to make a
collage around it? He keeps it out. He won't let me touch it.*

stuffed glass

> *...and use, to express yourself, the things in your environment, the images from your dreams, and the objects of your memory...*
>
> -Rainer Maria Rilke, from *Letters to a Young Poet*

in order of appearance:
camera.
three wine glasses given
as one wedding present.
camera grows, takes shots
of glasses that look plastic
that look safe
that won't break,
but camera refocuses on
crystal with a silver rim
they wobble on a cement floor
they might shatter beards of glass
they are empty, they are sad
they are temperamental little men
i stare, grieve
then see you unwrapping them
from glossy gray paper
and white tissue
in an apartment expiring
in two weeks and i laugh
celebrate my new home
then out of your home

you put your hands on my shoulders
you put your shoulders on my hands
you will hold me will you
get back together again
back together back to
glasses without red or white
instead, they hold us dancing
you, in a starched white shirt
tight jeans and penny loafers
my clothes are breathless,
awkward i try to learn
the pony, mashed potato
all the dances of your era
on our first date at valleydale
the spotlight, our sun
everything else black
we are dancing in my apartment
we are dancing our second week
of marriage, in our kitchen
your cupboards resist
holding dozens of water glasses,
wine, champagne can't take this
mix, don't buy this silver lining
the last champagne falls
lands in one palm
i grab the bottom
the rest takes off
i cry, you tenderly pick the stem

left in my hand, kiss my forehead
lift pieces from white tile
floor your mother screams
from our family room, runs
to scold you for being clumsy
when i did it i did it
i must be dizzy
it must be the two-day honeymoon
or the dancing
or three people crammed
into a slender glass
or having to be quiet in bed
or the distraction of
the little men mumbling
swearing behind cupboard doors
with loose handles
or maybe it's the camera
or the dream
the confusion of
a picture deceiving
pretty

The Painter

Last Spring, he pledged himself
to small, household projects.
Their upstairs hallway painted peach,
he covered his fist holes,
and gingerly brushed around the
scuffed, loose railing.

This Spring, the entire home
is his canvas.
He chooses a creamy ivory
for every room, every wall
the empty master bedroom
his first consideration.

He coats the wall
where the white iron bed he discarded
left a year's worth of marks,
then covers the nail holes,
from their framed wedding invitation
yanks out the hook that hung their honeymoon picture.

Eager to preserve each corner
of his room, he moves his dresser
discovers a check never cashed
a gift for their single anniversary

then lays it on top of loose change,
abandoned bobby pins.

His hands so meticulous, unmessy
he finds comfort, control
through each stroke
not mindful of the paint
that splattered dry on his ring.

He works diligently filling
the cracks and sees a smooth finish.
Loving the fix of his latex high
he paints one wall after another
away from recognition.

As Is

Scarlet cruet with stopper intact: first separation purchase
at *No Mistake* antiques. His instinct sniffs what's new
in her apartment, scolds her use of severance money
for something she doesn't need, as he places the glass tear drop
between his thumb and forefinger, gently removes it from
the bottle, inserts it into the small hole, removes, inserts,
methodical as his rehearsed smile.

But she does need it, more than rent money, more
than bread. Her first investment
between the absence in marriage
and the absence out of marriage.

Other stoppers minus foundations fill a ruby-lidded crystal box,
not fitting in neat unison, not serving purpose,
just space.

She's intrigued by pieces severed,
the holes, wrinkles, abyss,
the between,
interested in yielding to what's broken.

There's a tile missing in the bathroom
at Cambridge's Colonel Taylor Inn;
a hairline crack routes its way across
remaining map of wall. The owners understand
reverence in no repair,

that it is equally honorable to disavow polish for
    scratches, to see line
as adornment, in symphony with
the doily and candy dish,

the stain, chipped frame, water necklace drips,
the bottle's lip without body, lampless shade, gnawed
    chair arm
the knob divorced from dresser,
the one subsisting drawer;

our lives clue why things dissipate;
those things dissolute intimate our lives --
our scars, our cuts, our stitches; all
evidence of void, of residue
what breeds qualm, breeds attribute,

what marks sustain, evoke movement
maintain, as is.

Odd Pair

Since our best man became your roommate, and a woman called me
announcing she is your disgruntled girlfriend, it was a pretty good
bet your soap opera line, *I just need to get my head together,*
along with
this is only a trial separation. You'll move back in no time,
was total farce.

You wouldn't allow us to grow into our husband and wife tags,
yet ironically pushed for an October wedding,
even when I suggested late Spring, so you could iron out
daunting work accusations while resolutely
making your political name.

*We'll use one lawyer –my friend, Jim Smith -- get an easy
dissolution.*
We'll save so much money and finish this in no time.

I accept finale is near but will not agree to your modus operandi.
I didn't get married so you could flip me
a cheap and easy denouement months later; I won't pretend
we woke up with an identical amiable epiphany,
that we envision the same disunion, so soon after sealing a union.
You want to end it? Divorce me, and a baked fury sears the tip
of your nose, slashes color on your neck,
your fingertips florid when I tell you I'll get my own lawyer,
as if I know how, how to afford one, then

a colleague suggests the perfect barrister,
hands me a note card with the word *Kitten* and a phone number.
She reads my mind, says that is indeed her first name, fills me in
on her background. She's a former English teacher – used to teach
at our school, aspired another degree to be an advocate for women
who suffer marriage's demise, a plight for which she can empathize.
I end up with a former English teacher turned lawyer, who
used to work at my school?
What are the odds, or the

odds that I walk into her office and a non-descript woman
    in a white blouse
and beige skirt, gets down to business without rehearsal,
    implores
me immediately talk a spell before even offering me a seat,
weave the tail of our marriage, what heralds
our demise: *Don't give me any names, just talk. Talk,*
and her eyes close in concentration, as if listening to a
    symphony in aural search,
counting the wrong notes, and my face enflames at her
    command,

a nasal septum combustible with stories

molten larynx hot with buildup, even in scared monotone,
an anatomy devoid tenderness, and odds again, her eyes flare open
and she interrupts. An eruption of ugly spews from her mouth:

That goddamn mother fuckin' cock-sucker!

I'll destroy him, she says. She jolts me, calls you by name,
recognizes
threads in this narrative, because she is friends with your first wife.
What. Are. The. Odds.
*We'll make things so difficult for him. I'll see to it you'll get a hefty
alimony.*
I'll strip him his house. Yes. You will own his house, in no time.

I don't want his house! I blurt.

I tell her I want nothing. I don't want to ruin you. I only insist
you direct the divorce.
I wanted your love. Didn't get it. I want to part quickly, peacefully.

She pauses a slow, labored stare down. *Such an odd one, you are,* she says.

A Matter of Semantics

She will not give him a dissolution,
says she didn't marry him, only to
part less than two years later.
She says he'll have to divorce her,
and she waits for papers to come
in the mail. They never do,
and her lawyer calls his;
he says his client can't file because he has no grounds,
that her client did nothing wrong.
So he waits it out until she
must come up with her own,
but all she did was talk to her lawyer, until she
gets a copy of her own charges in the mail,
gross neglect and extreme mental cruelty,
and she cries, worries her soon-to-be ex
will be highly offended by this, not aware that
her lawyer wears pragmatic glasses, examines
two charges as logistical mortar for all her woeful narratives
and crafts them formal and efficient, for a special delivery
man to place them in her husband's hands.

When she calls to check on his feelings, his response
is phlegmatic: *Why are you upset? Gross neglect.*
That's what it is. Hmmm... I'm not sure about the
extreme mental cruelty. Let me think about that one...

The Key In

Use of your key
is about to expire.
I keep it as many evenings as
I can to collect scattered residue of mine,
to walk about smelling
each opening
of each room, while I can
still finger the scope of
this home, while I am
still in contract with
you, under your roof.
It was never our roof,
since you never added my name
once we married.

Some would think
meandering just before divorce
asks for deeper grief.
Why would I choose to taste
another dour bite of a dwelling
pushing my vacancy?

Perhaps that's why pain
remains jagged
with edges and textures
never smoothed over,
always wanting to examine

what happened, instead of
getting a head start on murmurs
of air more inviting, accepting.

But, any clues why you
want me out have got to
be soaking inside some left-over shadow
here. I'm so close, I hear it.

Five out of five had
diagnosed our malady --
the therapist, psychiatrist,
sex therapist, Christian counselor
and Methodist minister – identically.
But I want only your words to penetrate me,
what you surmise makes me an aversion.
Once I receive them, I can really change
or move on. I don't need to like the answers.
I just need answers willing to come to
all my rooms inside me ready,
waiting, welcoming to receive.

I step to your opened office door.
On your library desktop, a book
is opened but face down.

Without hesitation, shame, I lift
it, see what it is. It's a journal entry
from the day before:
> Sandy's gone. Shall I tell her the truth?
> We shall see how it makes me feel.

In Grandpa's Cellar

June of '89 I visited
waving my emerald engagement ring
like a handkerchief flirting,
teasing you, the race on,
I'd try to beat your fifty-eight-year record.
Two Junes later
I'm back in New England
with nothing left but rings.
You've never met my husband.
You never will.
You don't ask questions, instead
you take me down the cellar stairs
past what's left of Grandma's
canned goods, twist the single
light bulb illumine crates of old bottles.
You and Grandma spent year twenty-six
collecting cruets from
discarded homes, and vials
and apothecary jars from flea markets
sold them to make your way
across the United States and back.
Knees and feet dirty
from damp earth floor,
I indulge in what's left
of your 1955 adventure,

wipe webs from amber and aqua
and Lydia Pinkham
and escape to forget a love
that didn't last
and you escape to remember a love death severed.
I take them upstairs five at a time
plop them in hot soap bubbles
scrub them shiny, ready to wrap,
find them places in my new apartment.
One crate remains in your cellar.

Incoming Male

One afternoon junk mail conceal three personal letters
in her mailbox for a short interlude, epistles patiently
anticipate her attention, in the teacher's mailroom.

Words impending divorce become her virtual nametag
and like a large one announcing a teacher at open house, imagine
it passing through teens' hands, through their voices,
mixing into a hallway maelstrom, gaining momentum to land
as a centerpiece of talk on a teachers' lounge table.

Remember this: before cell phones' instant texts and tweets
the etiquette of reflection; glory in effort, decorum in a pen,
lettered care. Paper folded, creased, envelopes sealed for
simmering emphasis after rumor creates impetus:
one piece of folded notebook paper, a letter from a senior
student who states her age difference miniscule, when he
graduates, a date he desires. Two envelopes: the first,

from a teacher whose habitual lechery came to a halt
when she married; he pronounces his inclination to resume
flirtation. He wants to show her his real estate. Buy her coffee,
graduate to stronger libations. And final envelope:

a student's father introduces himself directly after
his salutation. Bold cursive strokes speak of his sophomore
son in her seventh period class coming home one day

announcing her near availability. Would she be willing to give it a shot with him? He's a widower with four kids he can't take care of on his own. He owns his home — doesn't rent. A half block from school, she could walk to work— the situation, ideal.

You Still Married?

It was strange enough that the Judge's last name was Cloud.
I don't know why. It just was,

and unfair enough that I was the one who showed
up for the divorce and he didn't.
It felt like he didn't even care enough
to watch the ending, to man up to what he wanted,

and it was bad enough that my lawyer told me to
act extra meek, that I had to speak softly, and very nicely
ask for my last name back.
She said the judge was extra-conservative
and might not grant me my request.
*But I legally hyphenated my name. I have to endure this caveman
routine to remove a simple hyphen and his name?*
Yes.

The judge granted my last name's weight loss.
The worst thing wasn't even this archaic scenario.
No, when I was walking across the courtroom parking
lot, a student named Dale just happened to be at the other
end. We both had him for a student. I can't
imagine why he would have been there.
Why would he have been there?

He yelled across the parking lot, loud as sunshine:
Hey! You still married to Jones?
I looked at my watch. I don't know why
I looked at my watch. *For about 20 more minutes,*
then turned and went into the courthouse.

Now, that was the worst.

An Average Woman's Addiction to Chocolate

Anthony Thomas lives in my neighborhood.
I visit him at least twice a week.
He entices me with inexpensive
sweet slips. It is my choice:
cordial cherry, double dark fudge,
butter cream mistakes.
I stop by on the way to my therapist,
back from the dry cleaner,
often before and after church
and my car is littered
with midget cupcake wrappers
before I even reach my destination.

Sometimes I'm a real chocolate junky.
I'll forget trying to get fat with class.
Rite Aid sells boxes of bridge mix for $1.09,
and there are always candy bars in Kroger's
all-night checkout.

I've gained fifteen pounds since I was first
separated, just over a year of gut slowly
jutting under the dress belt.
I suck in as hard as I can
while taking attendance in study hall,
because students whisper
I'm not as pretty as I used to be.

My first gift to myself just after surviving
the courtroom was a treat from The French Loaf.
*Give me the most fattening thing you make
with the most chocolate,* I request.
Are you celebrating something? the baker asks,
handing me an eleven-layer chocolate torte.
Well, I deserve something sweet.

And one of your first gifts to me were Lady Godiva
chocolates. We fed them to each other —
fingers and candy touched each other's lips
then lingered, playful on our tongues.
You teased me, said when we married, you'd eat them
off of me. You were a tease.
You bought me chocolate bon bons each time
we registered for wedding presents.
As your wife, you told me how fat I am.

The first time I talk to you since our divorce
you say you're still seeing that woman named Monique.
Your voice has that soft catch, your sign
that spells love I remember so well.
I ask you what she looks like.
Not to worry, you say,
*She isn't petite — not even thin.
She's just average, like you.*

Divorced Girl's Rant

Make me eyes for a mug handle
make me eyes for this pen tip
make me eyes for my hangnail
and eyes for my bracelet hook
and eyes for his freckles
and eyes for the film
clouding the window
and eyes for the lines
dividing toilet paper squares.
Make me eyes for my legs
and legs for my eyes, and feet
to carry my eyes to the depth
of his brain so he can see
through my eyes a woman
with pits in her face
he ruined he ruined
he blinded for life.

1991 AIDS Test Debacle

Everyone urged her.
All it takes is just one time,
this acronym fate.

She asks, nurse eyes why.
She should not have to explain
but does, nurse exits.

Hallway whispers her.
She hears it, one door between
She waits, they gossip.

Blood taken, days drag,
answering machine records
nurse's call. *Urgent.*

Please call back, nurse states.
She rewinds cassette, replays.
Demise, evident.

She is put on hold.
*We regret to inform you
the chemist suffered*

*a serious fall.
A tray of blood vials he held
flew up in the air*

*when his left ankle
turned, collapsed, but he managed
to catch all the tubes*

*midair, save, but yours.
So come back and we'll retest
No mishap this time.*

No phone shares outcome.
Much later results from un-
likely source, her ex,

who mails her private
worry through inter-office
school mail, first sent by

mistake to his house,
though she made clear that she moved.
He had a post-it

next to prognosis
an incredulous, *Really?*
as if wronged, injured.

She calls the doctor
politely points out this breach
to head office nurse.

*We can't keep track of
people like you who are in
and out of homes and*

*marriages so fast.
There is no guarantee it
won't happen again.*

Content

This Christmas
there will be no mantle
for rocking horses' prance, no stage
of little white lights,
yet they will still unwrap
themselves from tissue

announce stain glass, wood,
red iron on top of china cabinet
graze English Ivy, Philodendron
lining apartment bay window
rhythm side by side rocker
lean to Sadie as she rubs
chin on manes.

We will still celebrate
smell of pine
eat sugars, tuna
on ruby red plates
sip cinnamon, blackberry teas
in bubble glass cups.

We'll hum *sleep in heavenly peace*
play *Somewhere in Time*
burn rose potpourri
light red and green candles
dress tree with ivory lace, while

that mantle remains empty of memory
walls, pictureless
kitchen window, curtainless

and he lies in bed
divorced contact, conversation,
commotion, clamor, chaos,
no more clutter.

Lost Suitcase

Our suitcase has been wandering aimlessly for four years now.
We landed that spring break in Key West without our belongings.

When our luggage paid with wedding money never arrived,
we filed the first claim, the second, then the third from home.

Six months later Delta signed a $300 check, a letter of apology.
The money didn't cover your brand new contact lenses,

my sundress that still wore tags, the bathing suits, swimming
trunks, dancing pumps and pink negligee.
It didn't come close, nor

did your settlement check ten months later
cover the damage, fist holes, kissless indifferent nights.

You paid, literally, your last visit, and with no letter of apology.
You handed me the long envelope as if I won the lottery

or got to read the Oscar for best actor:

> *You'll just love this.*
> *Buy something nice for yourself,* you said, relieved,

like someone paying off a long overdue library fee,
and tears have me.
> *But I'm giving it to you a month early!*
> *I thought you'd be excited,*

and you backed to the door, like a kid

feeling he was being scolded for something
he didn't mean to do.

Your goodbye teetered, like a wine glass missing the tabletop,
grazing the edge when you glanced at my antique desk,

with all its books that once sat in our family room.
I held onto you, sudden, urgent, my head tight to your chest,

I tried to hear whatever memory held you hostage for one second,
but I blinked, felt a pillow, feathered and weightless.

You left, I put the check in the bank, let the dollars fly out
like New Year's Eve confetti thrown, then swept away,

like wedding rice scattered everywhere,
like a lost suitcase found.

Who might be more curious—someone opening a treasure chest
from the other side of the world,

or we, finding abandoned love on our doorsteps?
Maybe the suitcase still wanders, a vagabond, its lock
    suffocating old promise

just like a firefly caught in a clear plastic container.
The next morning the light, gone.

Meat and Bone

You were my Sweetmeat, most often, shortened to Meat,
a nickname I gave you when you introduced me
to antique auctions, and the time
we heard two hours of vigorous bidding
during one, dealers battling for Victorian porcelain sweetmeats:
intricately designed candy dishes meant for
sweet delicacies, pastries, fine candied fruits.

14 years my senior, I laughed, said you were my favorite
antique, my yummy confectionary I always craved.
You quickly satisfied my longings, dizzying me with your
affection, filling my every romantic whim: your love notes,
long, slow appetizer and dessert kisses, playing hide and
seek in your house, George Winston's piano
music glossing the background of candlelit dinners,
I didn't sleep much, so charged
on the cotton candy fix of you
before we married.

Just after, you named me Bone,
and I thought it was because of the weight
I dropped that Fall, even though there wasn't much
to lose. But I was beginning
to fit into size 4s, surely because of our running three miles
as many days as you fit into our schedule, and you trained me
to eat no more than half a sandwich. I cut off all my *Rapunzel* hair,
as you called it, cropped it short like a boy's
just like you said you really wanted.

But you said I had it all wrong.
Bone was short for Lazy bone, because you said
my energy level was low for someone in her twenties.
You couldn't understand why my body wasn't limber enough
on your Nordictrack, why I squirmed when you pressed my chest
so my back went down to the bench, forcing me to bend back
    further than I could.
You claimed lack of motivation made me yell. Not pain,
and bonafide laziness wouldn't organize all the labels on cans
to face the same direction in our kitchen pantry, the way you
    wanted.
Rooms should be dusted, and laundry baskets emptied in
    unison,
and I never grade my papers fast enough. Despite your charges,
I loved my nickname,

because even when physical affection
left our marriage the moment we stepped in it,
I heard endearment in your voice, every time you called me
    Bone,
or at least its residue. That's what I told myself anyway,
to the point that I wanted you to attach *Lazy*
to it and give me the full-blown negative nickname,
simply because I'd get two more syllables of
vocal bliss directed toward me.

So one night we had one of our horrible fights,
and I left. Instead of driving
around for a typical twenty-minute cool off,

I popped
into the all-night Meijer near us, wandered
to their small pet department
sandwiched between sapped roses on sale with
remnants of black-eyed Susans wearying their petals on tile floor,
and a bin of baseball bats and camping gear.
I spotted two plump, orange goldfish,
eyes beaming, almost unnaturally bright bellies, as illuminous
as florescent lights blinking shopping guidance for night owls
in need; this the peace gift. The mug with the painted calico
identical to our Sadie, Godiva chocolate, and red tulips never
    soothed
past stings from arguments, but when I came home

with my fists holding together two bright lives swimming in
    plastic,
the bad cold you were brooding and chill of our unfinished
    business
dissipated. Your eyes dressed a boyish hope.
Like kids, we set out to bring the goldfish together in the best
matrimony of glass we could find. In unison, we announced

we'd name them Meat and Bone;
I squealed in delight.

For weeks we nurtured the pair,
decorated their meager bowl to commemorate their dominion
    of love.

You were as tender to their care
as you were to hunt for Sadie
who somehow got out without our realizing it.
You searched in earnest. Your steps foraged all
sidewalks and fields, to no avail, spent late nights
staring out despair's window, hoping to spot her,
and when she returned to our porch on her own terms a
    week later,
you scooped her up, your tears wet her head and whiskers and
hugged her, me, as hard and long as I will ever remember.

That was our first April, and 17 months later
the contract between us ended. Because you got a vehement no
after asking for visiting rights to my cat,
you insisted on keeping Meat and Bone together
and that was that.

Thirteen Years Later

I hear your mother died.
I call, offer condolences. I hoped time and soothing words
would create the salve we need.
You dredged up the dirt of our dead married selves, repeat
a performance that you just couldn't be married, and
your words percolate my neck to groin, impregnate their
throb in my cage. You still talk, conjure a wedding date
not ours. I tell you we hadn't even met yet; I was a college
student. Ache deepens, orchestrates my throat:
You don't remember when we married.

Thorny silence empowers
until memory manifests, snaps a finger-fast image
of something so small that once hurled us into
intimate water, diving deep,
albeit briefly. Remembering our goldfish

insight speaks, almost inaudible, questions in statements:
*Meat and Bone couldn't still be alive. How long. They lasted
   how long?*

You pause. Your tone shifts. Memory, precision speak:
*Meat lived seven years and five weeks after you left.
Bone died two days later. Thanks for asking.*

Complex

> *Our dreams draw blood from old sores.*
> - Ntozake Shange

A German Village apartment
newly rents me.
Paintings have not yet been
hung but a runner sits neatly
ironed on the buffet. Someone
is terrorizing women, chopping
off fingers. You call, you
just moved into an apartment
on the opposite side of my complex.
You have no running water;
you wish to shower in mine.
I keep waiting for you to come.
You don't.
I feel that old amalgam of charm, of dread.
Anxiety courts me and I am half drunk.
The pink Amish rug is trampled
by a plaid-suited, greasy-haired
man with a blade that will kill me.
Bathmats drip everywhere
and your parking lot runs into me
where you stand, long-haired
handsome yet, drying your ears
with a cheap blue beach towel;
you have the audacity to still
call me your bone.

You are freshly wet from
a shower that doesn't happen
in my provisional chamber, though you
asked for one earlier in casual desperation
and I cling to that conception
like knuckles bloodied in the
handicapped space, I thirst
informing you a killer is loose,
my time, limited, but my throat
restricts this exchange, ruminations
still soaked with hope you'll
belatedly transition into
my lit doorway. I crave
words evicted, but again they muffle
due to vexation of water trapped in your ear,
a bleary person's flipped hair several steps behind you:
a blade tip tickles my spine's lip.

Strange Things

Our things never had time to get comfortable with each other.
You appreciated my antiques but were more of a contemporary
aficionado, with your large glass coffee table on white stone, and
white couch and loveseat that nearly gave you a heart attack
when a friend's three-year-old was over and ran across both
in his tennis shoes.

Still, you were willing to experiment, placing my 1930s buffet
beside your white furniture, our wedding china in my china
   cabinet,
granted me full reign to decorate the mantle at Christmas time,
and your waterbed disappeared once I moved in.

But as months went by, your conversations on the phone
grew larger than time with me, and your mind
became a yours/mine map of stuff; *ours* dashed to the curb.

One day you bitched so much about my bags in our basement,
you demanded they had to go right then and there.
I crammed them in my car
drove 45 minutes and dumped them in my parents'
basement. You went along to help me, your 40 boxes
of pottery remaining in *your* basement.
While burdening my parents with 15 bags,
my mother said she was happy to take them if it was
going to help us have an easier, happier marriage.

You said nothing. Not even thanks.

When we separated, you asked to take one of the paired
abstract paintings my sister and her husband created
as our wedding gift. You said you would
certainly give it back to me if we didn't work out.
The painting has yet to be returned.

Because retracting was your new thing when I moved out,
some gifts from you were hidden from me:
goggles, swim fins, an orange glow in the dark waterproof
    watch, red high heels.
A month ago, a friend went to a garage sale and purchased
an oil painting that had been addressed on the back of it
to both of us on our wedding day.

But the strangest thing was attending a wedding shower.
The couple giving the shower were friends of yours.
I had taught with the man, was just getting to know his wife,
and she offered to give me a tour of their home.
Folk art we bought on our honeymoon announced itself
    on a dining room wall.
I asked if you gave it to them as a wedding gift. *Why yes,
    how did you know?*
I told her that it was just a hunch – that I simply know your
    taste so well.
Etched at the bottom it said, *Welcome to our home. There are
    no strangers here.*

June 3

She lingers on the phone with Lynn,
a friend she met decades ago,

on her first social date at Valleydale.
She liked her immediately, felt instant ease with her when
   they met,

and she recalls that he was eager to introduce her to his best
friend, Lynn's husband, who would become their best man,
just as he said he couldn't wait for her to meet his
other friends at a party he was already planning in his head,
where he'd announce her. He made his stairway her catwalk
and when she landed on the first floor of his home, his crowd
of friends met her and she, their approval.

But just as soon as he made first ballroom introductions
she remembers how he switched gears,
flawlessly performed the *Hitchhiker* and *The Swim*,
dances from an era she was only born into,
how his best friend nodded, looked on approvingly,
That was something, Boy, he said.

There was something extra special about
the fervor of their bond; within a year she'd marry
and she and Lynn would unite:

call their husbands' friendship the strongest
allegiance they'd ever seen; even as wives they
couldn't compete with the rhythm of that adulation.

Tonight, she lounges into the thirtieth year
of more phone conversations with Lynn
on her living room couch,
uncombed hair claiming one pillow and bare feet another,

recalls tonight is thirty-year anniversary of her engagement,
when he bought her a vintage emerald ring, something different,
during gallery hop night in the Short North;
she lost the ring about ten years after the divorce
and finally sold the wedding band last year – gave the money
to a wheelchair bound woman.

Lynn was there when he proposed to her, there when the rings
    disappeared
here to revere their soul sisters' syncopation.

Mockery of Mourning

Well, I'm sorry for your loss, you said,
to reciprocate my saying the same. What it took for me
to choke that out, what it took to come to this bereavement,
to bandy sympathy, look at you, pretend.

You wear the most stylish glasses, without mustache,
you are borderline gaunt, thinner each time I see you.
I am pleased you see me this thin, lament this thought
accumulates. You turn, accept a drink offered.

You have patches on your elbows, in fashion,
those literary ones I've always longed to see you adorn.
You've always dressed the way I love a man to dress, but
nothing beyond the look.

It is big of me to pull those words from the wardrobe, despite,
and big to let silence fatten our distance, rather than counter
your soldiering back my verbiage; thicker debt fits in your
language that never unfolds to fruition,

reason for ending a marriage, morsel of explanation,
apology, of a heads up that my clothes will be left in
a heaping pile, and his – the deceased – once infiltrating
my closet: belts invading, pants adjusting to stolen space,

nothing's straight, my moving day
one you marked a trial separation
his shirts and shoes crowding out
my last abiding hint of perfume.

Calling Hours

How many rooms rented for dead will call us back to each other?
Whether you speak to me or not (and you do,
whether you speak or not, and you speak)
embrace ensues: quick
formal, brusque, as a courtroom conclusion,
only from that room, you were absent.

You can't recall the year we married.
You think we married
before we even met. In our first eve
of someone's funeral,
amid roses overpowering death's fragrance,
you approach, shape courtesy for all to see,
and in seconds I see through you,
revisit an uninvited memory:
newly wedded, your surprise visit
at work caged in my head.
I loathe sham's throbbing recall; it won't
liquidate: love, pride seemingly ardent
that classroom shivered,

another funeral parlor, I hug walls surrounding
a fraternity of grief, to avoid your notice
nearly make it to that door open to life's air but you
abort conversation cut across the tears and sighs,

to tap me on my shoulder. I turn to your stare
and a delicate yesterday cradles between us: I'm standing,
holding your friend's baby, at a party we attended,
and in the center of that room smelling fresh with happy
parenting, you whisper, *Don't get used
to this. You and I will never have a child.*
I blink back to current melancholy, to your remark your hair
　is longer, as if I can't grasp the obvious,
and you look into my eyes, ask in breathless urgency,
Do you like it? Do you like my hair longer?

Nothing is vexatious and everything is.
There's no voiding myself
of frames that saturate then or now,
of tempestuous matter that levitates
above our names, separate in guest books
today, tomorrow, visiting the vanished,
but while years force us to meet inside more
space structured for commemorating loss,
an unconventional place to venerate, jars

routine: A mutual friend planned his own
calling hours at his favorite bar, the High Beck,
then his motorcycle roomed his death untimely.
I beat you to the maladroit play:
approach you, direct this stage having pre-rehearsed
in charge, say a little of nothing.
I smile casually, walk away first, whole with epiphany:
finally reaching the only closure:
that there is none

Epilogue

Thirty Years Later: But There Really Is
Closure.
It's called release:
Forgiveness.

FINAL EPILOGUE

A Drinking Song

Wine comes in at the mouth
And love comes in at the eye;
That's all we shall know for truth
Before we grow old and die.
I lift the glass to my mouth,
I look at you, and I sigh.

-William Butler Yeats

Sandra Feen is a member of the poetry troupe Concrete Wink, with Rikki Santer and Chuck Salmons. She has been a featured reader in venues in and out of Ohio for over 30 years as well as a former co-facilitator for several Columbus, Ohio reading series. In addition, she performs work by Holocaust writers in Susan Millard Schwarz's Anahata Music Project. A member of the Ohio Poetry Association, Bistro Poets, former associate editor of *Pudding Magazine* and former director of the Ohio Poetry Therapy Writers' Group, Sandy has a BFA in Creative Writing and a BS in English Education from Bowling Green State University, as well as an MA in Literature from Wright State University. She was one of twelve teachers selected for a National Endowment of the Arts first "Change Course" program through Wright State University's Institute on Writing and Its Teaching. Her most recent publications include 2019's *The Gasconade Review's Storm A'Comin'!* and The National Beat Poetry Foundation, Inc. *We Are Beat* 2019 Anthology. A collection of her poems was named finalist for *The Lascaux Review's* 2018 Lascaux Poetry Prize. Her book, *Fragile Capacities: School Poems* (NightBallet Press 2018) — nominated for the Ohioana Book Award—highlights her 32-year teaching career in an urban school system. The poem "Palms Monday" was nominated for a Pushcart Prize. She lives in Grove City, Ohio.

www.ingramcontent.com/pod-product-compliance
Lightning Source LLC
Chambersburg PA
CBHW020125130526
44591CB00032B/538